My mother and I had a nice long chat
about getting a pet like a dog or a cat.

But I told her, "I REALLY want a bat—
not a fish or a bird or a dog or a cat."

If I had a bat, I would name her Pat.
Her collar would say, "Pat the Bat."

I'd make her some supper—
two spiders, one gnat,
and all sorts of spooky bugs like that.

I'd pet her little head—pat, pat, pat.
I'd sing lullabies as she sat on her mat.

She'd sleep all day
with her wings folded flat—
I would always know
just where she was at!

But when the moon got round and fat,
she'd leave our bedroom habitat…

...and swoop out the window,
just like that—
to meet her pals,
a nice bunch of bats.

They'd flutter around like acrobats,
then sit in my tree for bat chitchats.

On Show-and-Tell Day,
I'd wear a tall hat,
and on my shoulder,
there'd be Pat!

At first some kids
might want her to scat,
but after a while,
they'd start to love Pat.

I REALLY hate to be a brat,
but I want a bat,
and that is that!

Try as I might, Mom said no to the bat.
So I'd like you to meet
my new cat...named Pat!

(-at) Word Family Riddles

Listen to the riddle sentences. Add the right letter or letters to the -at sound to finish each one.

1   When my kitten grows up she will be a ___at.

2   When it's cold outside I wear gloves, a scarf, and a ___at.

3   I saw a very big mouse. I think it must have been a ___at!

4   My cat eats so much that she is growing rather ___at.

5   The car could not move because the tire was ___at.

14

6 This is my high chair from when I was a baby. It's where I always __at.

7 My aunt calls on the phone each night so she and Mom can ___at.

8 I know my baseball mitt is in the yard, but I still can't find my __at.

9 The tiny bug buzzing in my ear is called a ____at.

10 Please wipe your feet on the __at.

Now make up some new riddle sentences using -at

Answers: 1. cat, 2. hat, 3. rat, 4. fat, 5. flat, 6. sat, 7. chat, 8. bat, 9. gnat, 10. mat

-at Cheer

Give a great holler, a cheer, a yell

For all of the words that we can spell

With an A and a T that make the sound –at,

You'll find it in mat and cat and bat.

Two little letters, that's all that we need

To make a whole family of words to read!

Make a list of other –at words. Then use them in the cheer!